THE EUCHARIST

Encounters with Jesus at the Table

Robert D. Cornwall

Topical Line Drives Series
Energion Publications
Gonzalez, Florida
2014

Cover Design: Henry Neufeld

ISBN10: 1-63199-011-X
ISBN13: 978-1-63199-011-3

Energion Publications
P. O. Box 841
Gonzalez, FL 32560

energionpubs.com
pubs@energion.com
850-525-3916

INTRODUCTION

Only a third grader at the time, I was invited to serve at the altar as an acolyte at St. Barnabas Episcopal Church of Dunsmuir, California. In ordinary circumstances I would have been too young to take up this duty, but we didn't have many children in this small church. Although I was really too small to see over the altar, and too young to be confirmed and thus able to receive the Eucharist, I assisted our new priest in his duties at the altar. Today I preside at the table of the Disciples of Christ church I serve as pastor. From that earliest experience at the table to my experiences today, the Eucharist (also known as Holy Communion, the Lord's Supper, or the Mass) has stood at the center of my worship experience. In this I am not alone. The Table of the Lord has from the very beginning been the place at which we expect to encounter Jesus, for it was in the breaking of bread at Emmaus that Jesus revealed himself to the two disciples with whom he had sojourned (Luke 24:28-35).

Although the Eucharist stands at the center of Christian worship, there are a great variety of theologies and practices present within the Christian community. For some it is a mere memorial of Jesus' last supper with his disciples. For others it is the place where one not only encounters Jesus' spiritual presence, but consumes his true body and true blood under the signs of bread and wine. Although rooted in the practices of the early Christians, time has witnessed considerable evolution, and with evolution comes diversity of practice and belief. In part due to differing perspectives, this diversity has created a situation where the meal which celebrates the life of one who practiced open table fellowship has become a place of exclusion rather than inclusion, disunity rather than unity.

My hope is this small book will serve to encourage a conversation that can help us better understand this meal, so all who gather at the table might encounter Jesus anew in this meal and as a result experience transformation. My hope, as well, is that we can create

1

a conversation which builds bridges rather than walls. While there have been significant ecumenical conversations seeking to achieve this goal, I hope to extend that conversation more broadly.

The Eucharist is recognized by most Christian communities to be a sacrament — that is, it is a visible sign of God's work of grace in our lives. While we are baptized only once, at the beginning of our Christian journey, the Eucharist is meant to be received frequently as spiritual nourishment for the ongoing journey of faith. In part due to the perception that frequent reception can lead to misuse and abuse, some traditions have shied away from frequent celebration of the Lord's Supper. While I understand the reasoning, I am an advocate of frequent communion. If worship is centered on Word and Sacrament, then should we not commune with God, and with each other, each time we gather to hear the Word of God read and proclaimed? But should we choose this pathway, it is important this supper not become a lifeless ritual, but rather a *life-giving* ritual.

Although there is great diversity in theology and practice, the Eucharist we celebrate today clearly has biblical roots. Christians look to Jesus' institution of the Supper on the night of his betrayal as the foundation for this meal. Paul wrote he had received from the Lord the call to the table, where bread and cup were shared in remembrance of Jesus. As they ate the bread and drank from this cup, they would "proclaim the Lord's death until he comes" (1 Corinthians 11:23-26). We also look (or should look) to Jesus' own table fellowship, where he dined with sinners and tax collectors, reminding us that Jesus' understanding of the table was an inclusive one. Looking to the Book of Acts, we see Table Fellowship was numbered among the practices which defined early Christian worship (Acts 2:42).

While there is agreement that the Eucharist is a meal of remembrance and thanksgiving, significant questions surround the idea of Christ's presence in or at the Communion experience. Is he present or is he absent? If present is he present in the elements or in the community? Such questions have served to divide the church down through the ages. However one answers the question, it is good to remember that Jesus promised to be present whenever two or three gathered in his name (Matthew 18:20). Surely this promise has some connection to what we do at the Table. Beyond questions surrounding the past and present, there is the further question relating to the way in which the Eucharist points us into the future. For Jesus not only promised to be with the church present on earth, but as we find revealed in the Book of Revelation there is the promise of a gathering of the saints at the messianic banquet Table (Revelation 19:9).

The various dimensions present in this meal call for a certain soberness and reverence, but they also invite us to join together in joyful praise. We may be called upon to remember the death of Jesus, but we are also called to remember the resurrection. This is not a funeral service, but a celebration of Jesus' continuing presence with us by the Holy Spirit As one of my favorite communion hymns puts it:

> I come with Joy, a child of God,
> forgiven, loved and free,
> the life of Jesus to recall
> in love laid down for me,
> in love laid down for me.

Then we sing about coming together as a "new community of love in Christ's communion bread" (Chalice Hymnal, 420). Alexander Campbell, a founder of my own faith tradition, recognized the need for the Table to be a joyous celebration, writing that "with sacred joy and blissful hope (we) hear the Savior say, 'This is my body broken — this my blood shed for you'." These signs of Christ's love for us excite within us a sense of joy and they stir in us a love for our neighbor.[1] Finally, the oneness of the bread and the cup remind us that we who are many are made one when we come to the table. So, when we invite the world to the table the Lord has set, we invite them to share in the blessings of his kingdom.

---

1 Alexander Campbell, *Christian Baptist*, 3 (Aug. 1, 1825): 175 (Reprint, College Press, 1983).

As we move through this brief study of the Lord's Supper I will be using three terms interchangeably — Eucharist, Lord's Supper, and Communion.[2] While they are in a sense synonymous, or at least point to the same event, each term has its own meaning and application and we need to keep this in mind.

The first term is "Lord's Supper." When we use this phrase, we are reminded that the meal we are sharing has its origins in the Last Supper Christ shared with his disciples. We continue to share this meal because Christ initiated it and ordained his followers to continue this practice until his return (1 Corinthians 11:23-26).

The second term is Eucharist, which derives its name from the Greek word for giving thanks — *eucharistia*. Although the idea of thanksgiving is definitely rooted in the New Testament teaching and practice, especially in Jesus' acts of thanksgiving in the Last Supper, the earliest references to the meal using this term is found in the Didache and the letters of Ignatius.

The third term or phrase is Holy Communion. This reference is rooted in the description of the meal in Acts as one of *koinonia* or fellowship. It speaks of both the fellowship we have with one another at the table and the fellowship or communion we have with God. The first aspect, *koinonia* with each other, is rooted in the fact that the early Christians probably celebrated the Lord's Supper as part of a larger agape feast, or potluck dinner. This idea is found as well in the sense of breaking of bread, the concept found most often in the book of Acts (Acts 2:42, 46). The idea of communion with God as part of the supper is brought out in 1 Corinthians 10:16, where Paul speaks of our communion with the risen Lord in the sharing of the supper.

If we can affirm the premise in which contemporary Eucharistic theologies and practices have evolved over time, then it would be appropriate to rehearse some of this development and then ask

---

2   I need to acknowledge that in the Roman Catholic tradition the Eucharistic service is often referred to as the Mass. While this isn't a term I normally use, we need to acknowledge its use in a significant portion of the Christian community.

how these developments influence current practice. This book is not meant to be seen as offering a definitive picture, but I do hope it stimulates a conversation that will enrich the spiritual journeys of those who join me on this Christian sojourn. My hope is this conversation leads to a richer experience at the Table and provides a foundation for a bridge to fuller communion across denominational lines

Toward these ends, in the course of this book, we will look at the sacrament from several vantage points. We will look at biblical roots, and then examine developments through the post-Apostolic Age, the Medieval period, and on to the Reformation. Moving forward to the present we will examine current trends and developments in light of this evolutionary reality.

CHAPTER ONE

BIBLICAL AND THEOLOGICAL FOUNDATIONS

We trace our practice of coming to the Lord's Table to Jesus' institution of the meal at the Last Supper. As he shared a final meal with his disciples, Jesus broke bread and shared a cup with them, and told them to continue this practice of Table Fellowship as a memorial to him. According to Paul's account, they were to do this until he returned (1 Corinthians 11:23-26). The "Words of Institution" provide us with an impetus to come to the Table, but if we're to fully understand the nature of this sacred meal, we must also keep in mind Jesus' much broader practice of table fellowship. We must ask how this practice impacts our vision of the supper.

Besides Jesus' institution of the meal and his own practice of table fellowship, we must view it in relationship to the Jewish observance of Passover. Although the Gospels are not in complete agreement as to whether Christ died on the Day of Passover or on the Eve of Passover, they are in agreement that Jesus died during Passover Week. To understand the meaning of this meal we now celebrate in remembrance of Christ's life, death, and resurrection, it is appropriate to begin with the Passover Meal.

PASSOVER ROOTS

The Synoptic Gospels teach us that on the night before he was to die on the cross, Jesus gathered his disciples to celebrate the Passover meal or Seder (Matthew 26:17-29; Mark 14:12-25; Luke 22:7-23; cf. 1 Corinthians 11:23-26). In the Gospel of John, this gathering occurred prior to the Passover, and John's Jesus doesn't provide us with words of institution. Instead, he washes the feet of the disciples and gives them a new command to love one another as he had loved them (John 13). While there is some differences in these pictures, all four Gospels place Jesus' final meal in a Passover context, therefore it would be appropriate to ask what the Jewish tradition might have to say to our own celebration.

We might start with remembering that the Passover meal commemorates God's act of deliverance of the people of Israel from their status as slaves in Egypt. In Exodus the people are told to "remember this day on which you came out of Egypt, out of the house of slavery, because the Lord brought you out from there by the strength of his hand; no unleavened bread shall be eaten" (Exodus 13:3). Each family was to observe this event annually as a remembrance. By sharing in this meal the Jewish people bear witness to God's acts of redemption which brought freedom to the people of God.

There is a liturgical element to the meal, as the people remembered this act of deliverance, which included breaking bread and sharing four cups of wine. Normally, the Passover was a family meal, and included the children. Although it's unlikely Jesus' disciples broke away from their traveling band to gather with their families, and while Christians do not celebrate communion in their homes, the Passover celebration was normally a family event. This has, I believe, implications for how we include children in the Eucharistic celebration.

At Passover, the children participated fully in the meal, even asking the questions that enabled the story of Passover to be told during the meal. Therefore, to exclude children from the table would be to exclude part of the body of Christ from the table fellowship of Jesus.

To extend this background story, we must remember the Passover is the beginning of the exodus from Egypt into the Promised Land. On the journey from Egypt to Canaan, God fed the people with manna. This was God's gift of sustenance — their daily bread. Jon Berquist writes that "Manna was God's sufficient, uncontrollable, unexplainable gift of life." It is a lesson in grace as well. When we gather at the Table, the lesson continues, teaching us about "a God whose gifts are sufficient for human needs." This gift of bread begins with the Passover, in which "God demonstrates the cost of such care and provision."[3] As we partake of bread and cup, in memory of Jesus, we are taken back to these stories of God's deliverance and provision, signs of God's grace to all.

A Meal of Remembrance

If the roots of the Lord's Supper are to be found in the Passover Meal, the meal as established by Jesus has several important meanings. The first image or idea attached to the meal is that of remembrance or memorial. As Jesus instituted the meal, he told the disciples to keep the Supper in remembrance of him (Matthew 26:17ff; Mark. 14ff; Luke 22:7ff; 1 Corinthians 11:23ff). The Greek word translated as remembrance is *anamnesis*, which has the sense of recalling something to mind. It is an act of remembering, but it is more than simply remembering something happened in time, as if one were to give a historical recitation.

Although many Protestants have followed the Reformer Ulrich Zwingli in insisting on a "bare memorial," this view is quite limiting. Markus Barth notes the Hebrew sense of the word of remembrance is far from a simple "intellectual or emotional recollection of an ancient event." Instead it serves as a celebration "that is, a public, common, dramatic, and festival expression of joy and gratitude for what God has done. Soul and body, the ear, the mouth, the stomach, the sentiments and actions of the participants are involved. Briefly, remembrance is an action of the faithful, an action destined to the praise and glory of a great deed by God."[4] It is, you might say, a re-engagement with Jesus' death on the cross and subsequent resurrection.

---

3   Jon L. Berquist, *Ancient Wine, New Wineskins: The Lord's Supper in Old Testament Perspective*, (St. Louis: Chalice Press, 1991), p. 28.

4   Markus Barth, *Rediscovering the Lord's Supper: Communicating with Israel, with Christ, and among the Guests*, (Atlanta: John Knox Press, 1988), p. 12

THE SUPPER AS ACT OF SACRIFICE

Rooted in the Passover celebration, the biblical account of the Lord's Supper incorporates the idea of sacrifice. Jesus is the perfect Lamb of God who has been sacrificed for us. "This is my body that is for you," Jesus says. "This is my blood." These words speak of sacrifice — an offering, an oblation of oneself for the other. In this sacrifice Jesus is the mediator of an atonement, a reconciling of humanity with God. He is, the author of 1 Peter writes, the one who ransomed us from our foolish ways with the "precious blood of Christ, like that of a lamb without defect or blemish" (1 Peter 1:17-19). This is clearly a reference to the Passover roots of the supper, and its remembrance of Jesus' death on the cross. Indeed, Paul speaks of Jesus as the Passover lamb who has been sacrificed for us, and therefore we are to keep the feast (1 Corinthians 5:7). The Lord's Supper is a festival of joy, hope and gratitude, not in spite of Christ's death, but because of it.[5]

SIGN OF THE NEW COVENANT

According to Paul, in instituting the Supper Jesus pronounces: "This cup is the new covenant in my blood" (1 Corinthians 11:25). Reference is made here to Jeremiah 31, where God tells Jeremiah that God will make a new covenant with Israel and Judah, one not written on stone tablets, but on the hearts of God's people (Jeremiah 31:31-34). The danger that confronts us is that we can interpret this new covenant idea in an anti-Jewish manner. That is, in Christ God has exchanged one people for another. It's as if God divorces the first wife and takes a younger bride. Such a view is inappropriate.

As we consider this idea of a new covenant, in the context of the message of Jeremiah 31, it is helpful to see in this, a work of God which helps us internalize the covenant God made with Abraham, a covenant of blessing. It is a vision, as Jon Berquist points out, where people are united "into a new community that

5   Barth, *Rediscovering the Lord's Supper*, p. 22

shares the vision of God and works together to make this vision happen." In this new community, "differences of gender, class, or position in life are erased; instead, those who most need the care of others receive it in the greatest degree. Control and power cease as helpful construction becomes the common goal. Responsibility increases in importance; sin and victimization are removed." These are the expressions of the new covenant, which we celebrate in the Eucharist.[6]

The new covenant is also a reflection of God's extension of the peoplehood of God to include non-Jews or Gentiles through Christ. The new covenant isn't another covenant made with a different partner; it's the restoration of that original relationship through the actions of Christ whose blood was "poured out for many." The word "many" refers (as early as Isaiah 53:11; cf. 52:15) not only to the sinners in Israel but also to the Gentile nations.[7]

ESCHATOLOGICAL IMAGES

The Eucharist carries an eschatological dimension, because it not only reminds us of the cross, but it points us forward into the future to the consummation of the reign of God in Christ's return to gather up the saints. Consider the tradition that Paul sought to pass on to us, a call to celebrate the meal of the Lord as a means of proclaiming his death "until he comes" (1 Corinthians 11:26). There is also Luke's account of the Last Supper, in which Jesus tells the disciples that he wouldn't eat again until his ministry is fulfilled in the Kingdom of God (Luke 22:16). Perhaps most presciently, we have the vision in Revelation of the eschatological banquet, the marriage supper of the Lamb (Revelation 19:9), to which our own meals with the Lord point.

---

6. Berquist, *Ancient Wine, New Winekins*, p. 133.
7   Barth, *Rediscovering the Lord's Supper*, 24-25

The Eucharist as a Communal Feast

In most congregations the Eucharist has been ritualized and focuses on the sharing of bread and cup. It would appear, from the reading of Scripture, that the earliest forms of this celebration took place in the context of a full community meal (Acts 2:42-48; 1 Corinthians 10-11). It is in the context of the meal that we see the ethical aspects of the Supper revealed. Thus, we read Paul's instructions — and rebuke — of the Corinthian church for their abuses of the supper. As a result, Paul calls upon the Corinthians to discern the body. Although this reference has been used to support the idea of Christ's real presence of Christ in the elements, the call to discern or recognize the presence of Christ's body more likely refers to the presence of Christ in the community itself. The Pauline admonition concerning hunger and sleep would support this conclusion. There are abuses — either in terms of overindulgence or in not receiving sufficient nourishment. This seems to be reference to a potluck supper gone horribly wrong. The admonition, therefore, calls on the community to make sure that Christ is honored by equalizing the sharing of food in the community. In other words, the way we treat others impacts our ability to commune with God (1 Corinthians 11:17-23).

The Eucharist as a Sign of Unity

It is unfortunate the Eucharist has become a meal of division. Because of doctrinal and institutional differences, the table is often closed to those outside a particular tradition. Many efforts have been made over the past century, including the work leading up to the publication of the Baptism, Eucharist, and Ministry Document in 1983. Sponsored by the World Council of Churches, this document is designed to reconcile Christian Eucharistic understandings and practices so that Christians might gather at the table of the Lord, affirming each other as brothers and sisters in the faith. We've not fully reached the point where the Table is truly a place of welcome for everyone, but there is biblical precedent for the table to be a sign of unity.

In his first letter to the Corinthians, Paul addresses the congregation's practice of table fellowship. Paul writes "because there is one bread, we who are many are one body, for we all partake of the one bread" (1 Corinthians 10:17). Contextually Paul shares his concern about moving from the table of the Lord to those of the pagan temples in Corinth, but I think the verse carries an important word to Christians — a reminder that when we share in the one loaf, we are mystically united with the entirety of the Body of Christ — both local and universal. Therefore, in our contemporary practice we might want to pay attention to the symbolism of our communion tables, as well as our words of welcome.

CHAPTER TWO

POST-APOSTOLIC DEVELOPMENTS

Our current practices and understandings of the Eucharist did not get passed down from the first century to the twenty-first century without any additions or changes being made to whatever existed in those earliest Christian communities. No one can claim to have the pure practice and theology of the first Christians. Adaptations have been made to fit new times and new places. Besides, there is no evidence that there was ever one authoritative tradition of Eucharistic theology or practice. We can't explore every development, but there are a few developments which have had special importance for Western Christians that need to be lifted up. We will focus on two important developments — the doctrines of Eucharistic sacrifice and real presence, because they often become points of contention and separation within the Christian community.

THE EUCHARIST AS A SACRIFICE

We have already seen that sacrificial language is present in New Testament descriptions of the Eucharist. Early in the second century, sacrificial language becomes more prominent. Consider, for instance, this word from 1 Clement (written about 100 C.E.): "For we shall be guilty of no slight sin if we eject from the episcopate men who have offered the sacrifices with innocence and holiness" (1 Clement 44:4). Sacrificial language is also present in the Didache (I'm of the opinion that it is a second century document):

> On every Lord's Day — his special day — come together and break bread and give thanks, first confessing your sins so that *your sacrifice may be pure.* Anyone at variance with his neighbor must not join you, until they are reconciled, lest *your sacrifice be defiled.* For it was of this sacrifice that the Lord said,

13

always and everywhere offer me a *pure sacrifice*; for I am a great king, says the Lord, and my name is marveled at by the nations (Didache 14:1-3).[8]

The concern here is that sacrifices offered as part of the Eucharist must be pure and undefiled. This language is clearly rooted in sacrificial practices described in the Hebrew Bible. Whatever they meant by this sacrificial offering, it does not appear that these early authors envisioned Christ's actual body being sacrificed on an altar. It's more likely these early writers are referring to offerings of praise or perhaps the representative offerings (oblation) of the bread and wine. A little later in the second century, Athenagoras distinguishes between the bloody sacrifices of the Jews and Pagans and the unbloody sacrifices of the Christians.[9]

We can see signs of change with the third century Carthaginian bishop Cyprian, who speaks of the priest/bishop offering sacrifices on the altar. In this context Cyprian connects the offering of the elements of communion with Christ's real presence, so that the Eucharist becomes an offering of Christ's passion.[10]

The fourth century bishop, Cyril of Jerusalem, takes the sacrificial imagery even further, envisioning the Eucharist as a propitiatory sacrifice. After the bread and wine are changed into Christ's body and blood:

---

8   *Quotations from Early Christian Fathers*, Cyril C. Richardson, ed., (New York: Macmillan Publishing Co., 1970). The italics are mine for emphasis.

9   Athenagoras, *A Plea for the Christians*, chapter XIII. http://www. earlychristianwritings.com/text/athenagoras-plea.html. In the 18th century Anglican theologian John Johnson spoke of this same distinction; See Robert D. Cornwall, *Visible and Apostolic: The Constitution of the Church in High Church and Non-Juror Thought*, (Newark: University of Delaware Press, 1993), 136-138.

10   S.v. "Sacrifice," by Everett Ferguson, in *Encyclopedia of Early Christianity*.

Then, after the spiritual sacrifice, the bloodless service, is completed, over that sacrifice of propitiation we entreat God for the common peace of the Churches, for the welfare of the world; for kings; for soldiers and allies; for the sick; for the afflicted; and, in a word, for all who stand in need of succour we all pray and offer this sacrifice (Lectures 5:8).

Although sacrificial language is used, the intent is that this is a spiritual sacrifice, and therefore an unbloody one. Nonetheless, through this sacrificial action the priest and people entreat God, asking God to apply the benefits of the sacrifice of Christ to their own lives. Cyril doesn't envision the priest sacrificing Christ physically anew, but he does seek to tap into the original sacrifice on the cross so that in the Eucharist the salvation promised by the cross can be communicated to the recipient.[11]

REAL PRESENCE AND THE EUCHARIST

Even as sacrificial language became more prominent during this early Christian era, so did the idea that Christ was truly present in the elements of the Communion service. These theologians sought to answer the question of what Jesus meant when he intoned: "this is my body"; and "this is my blood." Christians have wondered whether this should be taken as metaphor or more literally. Over time this language would be debated and developed, so that by the middle ages the literal had begun to displace the metaphorical and even the mystical.

We find discussions of presence as early as the writings of Ignatius (d. 117 CE). Responding to docetists (gnostic Christians) who denied that Christ came in the flesh, Ignatius insisted the bread and wine were truly Christ's body and blood. He accused the Gnostics of avoiding the Eucharist because they refused "to admit that the Eucharist is the flesh of our Savior Jesus Christ, which

---

11 Cyril of Jerusalem (2013-03-08). *The Catechetical Lectures of St. Cyril of Jerusalem* (Kindle Locations 6931-6934)

suffered for our sins and which, in his goodness, the Father raised" (Smyrnaeans 7:1).

Somewhat later, Justin Martyr spoke of the bread and wine in similar terms:

> For we do not receive these things as common bread or common drink; but as Jesus Christ our Savior being incarnate by God's word took flesh and blood for our salvation, so also we have been taught that the food consecrated by the word of prayer which comes from him, from which our flesh and blood are nourished by transformation, is the flesh and blood of that incarnate Jesus. (1st Apology, 66).[12]

Nearer the close of the second century, this sense of presence in the elements of the Eucharist becomes even more apparent in the writings of Irenaeus of Lyon:

> For when the mixed cup and the bread that has been prepared receive the Word of God, and become the Eucharist, the body and blood of Christ, and by these our flesh grows and is confirmed, how can they say that the flesh cannot receive the free gift of God, which is eternal life, since it is nourished by the body and blood of the Lord, and made a member of him? (Against Heresies, 5:3).[13]

The reference to the mixed cup speaks of the practice of mixing water with the wine. We can see in this a progression to a more developed sense of presence, but this does not rise to the doctrine of transubstantiation, an understanding of presence that develops much later.

Moving to the fourth century, we find an even more developed view of presence in the writings of Cyril of Jerusalem. He urges the readers to partake of Christ's body and blood in the figures of

---

12 Richardson, *Early Christian Fathers*, 286.
13 Richardson, *Early Christian Fathers*, 388.

the bread and wine. In that action, Cyril believed the participant became one body with Christ:

> For thus we come to bear Christ in us, because His body and blood are diffused through our members; thus it is that, according to the blessed Peter, *we become partakers of the divine nature*. (Catechesis, 4:3).

Still a question remains as to the means of transformation. Cyril advised his readers on this issue:

> Contemplate therefore the Bread and Wine not as bare elements, for they are, according the Lord's declaration the Body and Blood of Christ; for though sense suggests this to thee, let faith stablish thee. Judge not the matter from taste, but from faith be fully assured without misgiving, that though hast been vouchsafed the Body and Blood of Christ. (Catechesis, 4:5).[14]

While these early Christian leaders envisioned Christ being present in the Eucharist, they didn't specify how this took place. It is clear they were aided in their understanding by Platonic philosophy, which could envision a distinction between substance (Christ's body and blood) and what Plato called accidents (the elements of bread and wine). While the substance changed, the accidents remained what they had been. Even as the nature of the change was left undefined during these early centuries, there was disagreement between theologians in West and East over when the change occurred. In the Latin West the change was linked with the words of institution, whereas the Greek speaking East connected it to the prayer of invocation of the Spirit. In the second century, however, the Fathers believed that the Prayer of Thanksgiving as a whole consecrated the elements.[15]

One of the most divisive doctrinal developments has been the concept of transubstantiation. The question is, when did this idea

---

14   Cyril, *Lectures,* Kindle Location 6812.
15   Ferguson, "Eucharist," in *EEC.*

enter the picture? Whereas the idea of real presence has deep roots, the idea of transubstantiation is a rather late development, emerging as the Western Church entered the Middle Ages. As sacrificial language became more prominent and the language of presence became more realistic, theologians sought to go more deeply behind the mystery presented by these beliefs.

St. Augustine, writing in the fifth century, defined the sacrament as an external, tangible sign of a reality that existed only in the realm of the spirit. This meant that Christ was spiritually present in the Eucharist but not physically present. By the ninth century some theologians were thinking in more physical terms. Paschasius Radbertus (ca. 831) wrote an important treatise *De corpore et sanguine Domini*, which stated that after the consecration there was nothing there but the body and blood of Christ, though they could be found under the form of bread and wine. Thus the body that is received in the Eucharist is the same as that which was born of the Virgin Mary. Radbertus wrote:

> What is perceived externally is a figure or mark, but what is perceived internally is entirely reality and no figure at all; and therefore nothing else is here revealed but reality and the sacrament of the body itself—the true body of Christ, which was crucified and buried, surely the sacrament of his body, which is divinely consecrated by the priest above the altar with the word of Christ through the Spirit: whence the Lord Himself exclaims, 'this is my body' (Luke 22:19)."[16]

You can see the emphasis on physical presence. Although Radbertus' position did meet with opposition, especially from Ratramnus, who espoused a more symbolic and Augustinian view, Radbertus' position quickly became the dominant view within the Western Church.

---

16 Radbertus quoted in Bengt Hagglund, *History of Theology*, (St. Louis: Concordia Press, 1968), p. 156.

It was left to the Scholastic theologians, such as Peter Lombard and Thomas Aquinas, to fully develop this important doctrine that continues to define the Roman Catholic understanding of the Eucharist. These theologians set out to define the mechanism by which this transformation took place, giving it an authoritative definition.

Consider Peter Lombard's (1096-1164) understanding of the conversion of bread and wine into body and blood.

> To these we can reply as follows: That the body of Christ is not said to be made by the divine words in the sense that the very body formed when the Virgin conceived is formed again, but that the substance of bread or wine which formerly was the body or blood of Christ, is by the divine words made his body and blood. And therefore priests are said to make the body and blood of Christ, because by their ministry the substance of bread is made the flesh, and the substance of wine is made the blood of Christ; yet nothing is added to his body or blood, nor is the body or blood of Christ increased.[17]

A half century after Peter Lombard wrote, under the influence of Thomas Aquinas, The Fourth Lateran Council (1215 C.E.) gave official definition to the doctrine.

> There is one Universal Church of the faithful, outside of which there is absolutely no salvation. In which there is the same priest and sacrifice, Jesus Christ, whose body and blood are truly contained in the sacrament of the altar under the forms of bread and wine; the bread being changed (transubstantiatis) by the divine power into the body, and the wine into the blood, so that to realize the mystery of unity we may receive of him what he has received of us. And this sacrament no one can effect except the priest who has been duly ordained in accordance with the keys of the Church, which Jesus Christ himself gave to the Apostles and their successors.[18]

---

17 Peter Lombard in Ray C. Petry, *A History of Christianity*, 1:321.
18 "Canon I: the Creed, the Church, the Sacraments, and

It is important to note here the emphasis placed on the person who is entrusted with the responsibility of performing the actions that will lead to Christ's real presence being found in the elements of communion. The priest, duly ordained by a bishop, is the one entrusted with this work of the church.

The emphasis on Christ's real presence, as defined by the doctrine of Transubstantiation, and the doctrine of Eucharistic sacrifice led to the church taking the step of worshiping the host. If the host (bread) had truly become the divine body of Christ, then it, like Christ, ought to be worshiped. Thus the host was elevated and worshiped. Just being in the presence of the host was sufficient to cleanse one from one's sins. This meant the actual communion became unnecessary. In the host the person of Christ became tangible to the medieval masses.

CHAPTER THREE

THE EUCHARIST AND THE REFORMATION

Martin Luther and Ulrich Zwingli, two of the earliest Sixteenth Century Reformers, addressed the sacramental theologies and practices they inherited from the medieval church. They were in agreement that great abuses and misunderstandings had crept into the church. They were in agreement that something needed to be done to remedy this situation. However, they differed on both the theology of the Eucharist and the remedy to abuses. There is no better illustration of these differences than the debate that ensued between these two Reformers at the Marburg Colloquy, which was called together by Philip of Hesse, and met from October 1-3, 1529. The purpose was finding a means of bringing a sense of unity between the Saxon and Swiss reformers. Although the Colloquy failed to achieve its desired goal, it helped reveal the differences that had emerged among the Reformers. The Reformers agreed that the Roman Catholic doctrine of transubstantiation needed to be excised, but the way in which they reconstructed the doctrine of the Eucharist diverged considerably.

THE DEBATE AT MARBURG

It might be fitting to start with Martin Luther, whose doctrine of the Eucharist is often defined as "consubstantiation," though Luther never used this term. For Luther, the key to the debate was the interpretation of the words of institution found in the synoptic gospels (Matthew 26:26; Luke 22:19) as well as 1 Corinthians 11:24). Luther interpreted the Latin word *est* (is) in the phrase "this is my body" quite literally (does this sound strangely familiar? Does the meaning depend on the meaning of the word "is?"). Zwingli, the Reformer from Zurich, interpreted this little word much more metaphorically.

The story of the debates goes like this: Luther first debated the Reformed theologian Johannes Oecolampadius of Basel, while Zwingli debated Luther's colleague Philip Melanchton. On the second day, however, Zwingli and Luther faced each other. Before the other participants arrived, Luther entered the room and wrote in chalk on the table the words: "*Hoc est corpus meum.*" The debate went as follows:

Zwingli:
"It would be a shame to believe in such an important doctrine, teach, and defend it, and yet be unable or unwilling to cite a single Scripture passage to prove it."

Luther: (taking the cover from the inscription on the table)
"This is my Body! Here is our Scripture passage. You have not yet taken it from us, as you set out to do; we need no other. My dearest lords, since the words of my Lord Jesus Christ stand there, Hoc est corpus meum, I cannot truthfully pass over them, but must confess and believe that the body of Christ is there."

The disagreement that divided Zwingli and Luther is rooted in the way in which each interpreted the biblical text. Luther could affirm the symbolic nature of the elements, but he also believed these symbols did more than signify the presence of Christ. For him, the symbol contained that which it symbolized. While Luther rejected the Catholic understanding of literally eating the body and drinking the blood of Christ, he did believe in a mysterious way, the Christian partook of Christ's body and blood in the Lord's Supper. Luther, unlike Zwingli, took the word *est* (is) at face value, and as a result he retained a doctrine of real presence. The substance of the bread and wine may not change, but Christ did become present "in, with, and under" the elements of bread and wine.[19]

---

19 Timothy George, *Theology of the Reformers,* (Nashville: Broadman

Zwingli, on the other hand, insisted that *est* (is) meant "signified." Therefore, the Eucharist served to remind Christians of the event of the cross. He pointed Luther to passages of Scripture where Jesus referred to himself as a vine or a door. Surely Jesus didn't mean for these words to be taken literally. Zwingli found the key to his understanding in the words of John 6:63: "It is the spirit that gives life, the flesh is of no avail." Zwingli insisted, against Luther, that since the Spirit imparted salvation immediately there was no need for the "husks of externals." By distinguishing between body and soul, with the spiritual side being superior to the physical, Zwingli affirmed the primacy of the work of the Spirit. While the Spirit brought salvation and nourishment, the flesh brought very little. Therefore, one eats and drinks the elements of the Supper as a sign of thanksgiving for a work of grace already completed by the Spirit.

Why did Zwingli move in this direction? One of the major reasons was a concern about what he perceived to be a problem of idolatry. Even as he rejected images and the invocation of the saints, he had come to reject the Roman Catholic practice of venerating the Host and any doctrine that might encourage such practices. Therefore, he didn't believe Luther had gone far enough in alleviating this problem. To illustrate his point, Zwingli pointed to the relationship of the wedding ring to marriage. The ring may be a sign of the reality of a marriage, but it was not the same as marriage. Even so, the bread and wine signified the body and blood of Christ, but they were different from the body and blood of Christ. Thus, as one ate of the bread and drank of the cup, one remembered Christ's body and blood in one's mind.[20]

Both Luther and Zwingli affirmed the Chalcedonian doctrine of Christ's two natures — that he was fully human and fully divine. They differed in where they put their stress. Luther stressed the unity of the two natures, while Zwingli affirmed their distinction.

Press, 1988), pp. 150-53. David C. Steinmetz, *Luther in Context,* (Bloomington: University of Indiana Press, 1986), pp. 73-74.

20 George, *Theology of the Reformers,* 150-53. Steinmetz, *Luther in Context,* 73-76.

Luther talked about the ubiquity of Christ, that Christ could be everywhere, and therefore he could be "in, with, and under" the elements of bread and wine. The underlying doctrine is known as the *communicatio idomatum* (communication of properties). For Luther the interrelationship of humanity and divinity meant Christ could be present corporeally in more than one place, because his human nature had taken on the divine qualities of ubiquity in his resurrection and ascension. This meant that if Christ was present spiritually, he was also present corporeally. Therefore, whenever Christians eat the bread at the Lord's Supper, the body of Christ is present "in, with, and under" the elements.

Zwingli, however, took a much different view of Christ's corporeal existence. While Luther affirmed the ubiquity of Christ's physical presence, Zwingli emphasized the finiteness of Christ's physical presence. When the church gathered for the Eucharist, Christ was not present physically with the believers. He was, however, present with them spiritually by way of the Holy Spirit. For Zwingli, Christ's Eucharistic presence should be understood in terms of one's memory of Christ's act of sacrifice on the cross. It was an act of the mind, through which the reality of the cross was apprehended. Christ's body, however, has been seated at the right hand of God since the moment of the ascension, where he will remain until he returns in judgment.[21]

THOMAS CRANMER AND EUCHARISTIC PRESENCE

If Zwingli and Luther set out two Protestant poles of thinking on the Lord's Supper, and I use the word Protestant advisedly, Thomas Cranmer, Archbishop of Canterbury under Henry VIII and Edward VI, before being executed by Queen Mary, represents a middle ground. Cranmer's theology of the Eucharist came to be enshrined in the two Prayer Books that he largely composed and compiled, which have influenced Anglican and Episcopal liturgical

---

21 George, *Theology of the Reformers*, pp. 153-54. Steinmetz, *Luther in Context*, pp. 78-81.

practice up to the present. Like Luther and Zwingli, he rejected transubstantiation. Like Zwingli Cranmer rejected any sense of Christ's corporal presence either in or under the elements of bread and wine. Nonetheless, he continued to affirm a doctrine of real presence, which he understood both figuratively and spiritually.

Cranmer taught a view that has come to be known as receptionism. For him the elements of bread and wine sacramentally or figuratively exhibited to the participants in a concrete way the passion of Christ. The words "This is my Body" referred not to Christ's literal body but the bread, which was a figure of his body. Then, as the bread is eaten by faith, the recipient also receives the body of Christ.[22] The real presence therefore was found not in the elements, but in worthy reception of the elements by faith. In taking this view, Cranmer followed the medieval Augustinian theologian Ratramnus, believing that while the recipient received the symbols of Christ's body in the bread and wine, his soul fed spiritually upon Christ's body and blood.[23] He writes:

> The profession of the Catholic faith, is, that Christ (as concerning his bodily substance and nature of man) is in heaven, and not present here with us in earth. For the nature and property of a very body is to be in one place, and to occupy one place, and not to be everywhere, or in many places at one time.[24]

Although Christ was not corporeally present in the Eucharistic elements, Cranmer didn't follow Zwingli in believing that the elements were bare elements or tokens. Instead, he taught that God was present and working in the Eucharistic moment, bringing the fruit of grace to the participants in the Eucharistic service, as long

---

22 Thomas Cranmer, *Writings and Disputations of Thomas Cranmer*, 2 vols. Parker Society, Vols. 15-16. (Cambridge: Cambridge University Press, 1844), 15:15.

23 G. Dickens, *The English Reformation*, 2nd ed. (Penn State University Press), p. 186.

24 Cranmer, *Works*, 15:91-95.

as they received the elements by faith. Following the lead of Ra-tramnus, he taught when a person received the sacrament by faith the communicant received Christ's spiritual or sacramental body and blood. As one ate of the bread externally, one was inwardly, by faith, eating what nourished the soul to eternal life.[25]

Cranmer summed up his view of what happened in the eating and drinking of the Eucharist, holding that "in the true ministration of the Sacrament Christ is present spiritually, and so spiritually eat-en of them that be godly and spiritual." He denied that the ungodly in any way commune with Christ by partaking of the sacrament. He rejected corporal presence and sacrifice in contrast to spiritual presence and eating. He held that Christ was eaten spiritually "by believing and remembering Christ's benefits, and revolving them in our mind, believing that as bread and wine feed and nourish our bodies, so Christ feedeth and nourisheth our souls."[26]

Cranmer's theology of the Eucharist became enshrined in the two Prayer Books, the second of which took on a more Reformed hue. Long before his first *Book of Common Prayer* was published in 1549, Cranmer had been at work on devising new ways of turn-ing his Eucharistic theology into an appropriate liturgical form. It wasn't until after Henry died in 1545 that Cranmer was able to give full expression to his vision in the 1549 *Book of Common Prayer* and then later in the much more radical and Protestant *Book of Common Prayer* in 1552. In the second liturgy, Cranmer, influenced by the Continental Reformer Martin Bucer, who had recommended significant changes, simplified the Eucharist and eliminated all liturgical vestments, except for the surplice. Ordinary bread replaced the unleavened wafers of the Roman Church. He also split the service into three parts, and in doing so removed any hint of the sacrifice. He placed the prayers for the communion of the people before the consecration of the elements, implying that the consecration took place for the purpose of congregational com-munion. He had altars replaced with simple communion tables that

25 Cranmer, *Works*, 15:17.
26 Cranmer, *Works*, 15:203-204.

were placed in an east-west position with the priest standing on the north side facing the congregation. The words of administration were changed from "The body of our Lord Jesus Christ which was given for thee to preserve thy body and soul unto everlasting life" to "Take and eat this in remembrance that Christ died for thee, and feed on him in thy heart by faith with thanksgiving," giving it a more Zwinglian flavor.[27] Although the second *Book of Common Prayer* moved in a more Protestant direction, it did not completely follow Zwinglian lines. While the words of administration could imply only a commemorative and receptionist view, this did not directly contradict the Ratramnian view which Cranmer claims never to have given up.

---

27 Dickens, *English Reformation*, pp. 247-248.

CHAPTER FOUR

MODERN DEVELOPMENTS:
ECUMENICAL CONVERSATIONS

When we gather at the Lord's Table today to celebrate the Eucharist, the manner in which we do so, along with the theologies that underlie these practices, has a long history. In traveling from congregation to congregation, and from denomination to denomination, one will find both similarities and differences in Eucharistic practice and theology. In some places, the table will be open to all, while in others the table is open only to members in good standing. Depending on the faith community, one might find the congregation gathers at the table weekly, while others come to the table monthly or even quarterly. These choices can be rooted in theology, but sometimes they are simply a matter of habit or common practice. This is the way we've always done it.

Although this is but a brief exploration of the Eucharist, my intention is to draw lines from first century practices to the present. I have suggested that adaptation is to be expected. At the same time, it is important we keep in mind the biblical touchstones, asking how our current practices and beliefs measure up to what we find in the New Testament. This is not to say we can ever hope to fully restore New Testament practices. There might be good reasons why we don't do so. At the same time, it is important to keep continuity with these earliest practices. In other words, we're not free to do whatever we please with this sacred gift. Something new might emerge, but it emerges from some place.

If a person takes across the various Christian traditions, that person will discover that different faith communities emphasize different elements of the Eucharist. While one community may adopt a memorialistic understanding of the Supper — similar to that of Zwingli — others will highlight the Real Presence. But, as we have seen there are different understandings of real presence, so that one tradition might insist that after they are consecrated the substance of the bread and wine become the actual body and blood of Christ, while others locate that presence in the community. As for my own Eucharistic theology, I find Cramner's doctrine of a spiritual presence to be found in the community to be most attractive, although I am an ordained minister within the Christian Church (Disciples of Christ) which has historically tended toward the bare memorialism of Zwingli. This view fit nicely with the its Enlightenment sensitivities that accompanied the birth of the Disciples of Christ tradition. Interestingly, engagement with the Ecumenical movement and the liturgical renewal movement has led at least some Disciples to move beyond a Zwingli.[28]

In contemporary conversations about the Eucharistic, especially moving from theology to liturgical practice, there has been an effort to emphasize the role of thanksgiving. The word Eucharist reflects the Greek for giving thanks, and a focal point of many liturgies is the Prayer of Great Thanksgiving. In his own act of institution, Jesus took bread, blessed it and gave thanks to God before sharing it. As Ruth Duck suggests, this meal is not a funeral service (a mere memorial), it is a "meal of thanksgiving in which we give thanks for the presence of Jesus the Christ not only at the Table, but in our daily lives with their joy and trouble."[29]

The stress on thanksgiving goes together with questions about sacrificial imagery. Concerns have been raised in recent years about

---

28 Although broader understandings of eucharistic presence are increasingly present among Disciples clergy, that is less true of Disciples Elders who are typically charged with offering the prayer at the Table. These prayers typically focus on remembering Jesus' death on the cross for our sins, while providing little sense that the living Christ is present in or at the meal.

29 Ruth C. Duck, *Worship for the Whole People of God: Vital Worship for the 21st Century*, (Louisville: Westminster John Knox Press, 2013), p. 186.

the connection of the Communion and the prevalence of substitutionary atonement theologies that have proven problematic for many Christians. What do we mean by the claim that Jesus died for our sins and how does such a theology relate to what we're doing at the Table? Beyond this question there is concern, especially among feminist theologians, about violent imagery and the idealization of the sacrificial victim, which has been used to support oppression of women and others who find themselves living on the margins. We need to ask ourselves, as we celebrate this feast of God, what implications are present in our words and practice. Our answers must reflect sound theological thinking. This does not mean all sacrificial language must be abandoned, but it must be used with great care.[30]

Over the past half-century a great deal of attention has been given to liturgical theology and practice. Ecumenical conversations have focused on sacramental practices and theologies, as Christian communities have tried to find ways of bridging differences so that intercommunion can take place. Although the fences which separated Christians from each other at the table have been coming down, there are still barriers. Interestingly, the barriers tend to be the concern of church officials, not the laity. At the grassroots level, large numbers of Christians have chosen to take down the barriers themselves, often following in the footsteps of Jesus who extended table fellowship broadly — to whoever would come, including those whom society deemed sinners.

Although these grassroots efforts have their place, there is still a need to work out the differences which separate traditions. Therefore, several denominations have negotiated intercommunion pacts. For instance Lutherans and Episcopalians signed a Concordat in 1999 that reconciled theologies and liturgies. The United Church of Christ has a partnership relationship with the Christian Church (Disciples of Christ) and has signed agreements of full communion with the Evangelical Lutheran Church of America,

30 Ruth Duck provides a brief, but helpful discussion of this issue in *Worship for the Whole People of God*, pp. 201-204.

the Presbyterian Church (USA), and the Reformed Church of America. Another effort at promoting intercommunion has been the Churches Uniting in Christ, which emerged out of the Consultation on Church Union. The nine Protestant denominations who are members have committed themselves to the recognition of each other's baptisms and the commitment to share communion together. While officially intercommunion does not exist between Protestants and Catholics, it does occur informally — sometimes with the blessings of priests.

With regard to efforts at creating opportunities for intercommunion, one would be remiss in not mentioning the work of the Faith and Order Commission of the World Council of Churches. In 1983 this body produced a major groundbreaking document entitled the *Baptism, Eucharist, and Ministry Document*. A key statement from paragraph 19 of this document states:

> The eucharistic communion with Christ who nourishes the body of Christ which is the Church. The sharing in one bread and the common cup in a given place demonstrates and effects the oneness of the sharers with Christ and with their fellow sharers in all times and places. It is in the Eucharist that the community of God's people is fully manifested. Eucharistic celebrations always have to do with the whole church, and the whole Church is involved in each local eucharistic celebration. In so far as a church claims to be a manifestation of the whole church, it will take care to order its own life in ways which take seriously the interests and concerns of other churches.[31]

Although there remain important barriers to full communion — such as the role of the historic episcopate — the creators of this document recognized true unity will not be realized until Christians are able to gather together at the Open Table of the Lord

31 http://www.oikoumene.org/en/resources/documents/wcc-commissions/faith-and-order-commission/i-unity-the-church-and-its-mission/baptism-eucharist-and-ministry-faith-and-order-paper-no-111-the-lima-text

as one body in Christ. The message to the churches is that what congregations do on Sunday mornings at their own tables should be a sign of Christ's presence in the church in all its manifestations across the globe.

CONCLUDING THOUGHTS

We are the inheritors of a rich legacy of Eucharistic thought and practice. Although we have often found ourselves separated from each other at the Table of unity, if we're open to hearing the voices of our spiritual ancestors offering to us words of wisdom perhaps we can gather at the table and learn from each other. There is value in recognizing what Orthodox and Roman Catholic theologians say about sacrifice. And real presence can enrich liturgies that tend toward mere memorialism and exclude the presence of Christ from the liturgy. At the same time, the memorialism of Zwingli can warn against pushing Eucharistic thought into superstition and magic. We can learn from persons like Ratramnus, John Calvin, and Thomas Cranmer, who sought to find a middle way which included both remembrance of the earthly ministry of Jesus, and Christ's presence in our midst now. As we talk with each other, we may discover that Luther and Calvin were much closer than we realized. We may also find a liturgy centered in both Word and Sacrament is richer than one focused on one at the expense of the other. We can also learn from feminist theologians, who have raised important questions about the social implications of words and practices.

In writing this brief exposition of the Eucharist, my hope is that it will lead us all to having a conversation which will enrich our own faith and practice, as well as building a bridge that will lead us to find the unity of the body of Christ at the table of the Lord, a table Jesus invited us to gather at in his memory until his return. My hope is that by reflecting on both the biblical witness regarding the Eucharist, including Jesus' practice of table fellowship, together with the developments and adaptations that have occurred over time, the Christian community as a whole might see the value of coming together at the table with frequency, even weekly if not more often. If, as I believe, Holy Communion provides nourishment for the spirit, even as food nourishes the body, then we should not stay away from the Table Jesus spreads out before us.

TOPICAL LINE DRIVES

Straight to the Point in under 44 Pages

All Topical Line Drives volumes are priced at $4.99 print and 99¢ in all ebook formats.

Available

The Authorship of Hebrews: The Case for Paul	David Alan Black
What Protestants Need to Know about Roman Catholics	Robert LaRochelle
What Roman Catholics Need to Know about Protestants	Robert LaRochelle
Forgiveness: Finding Freedom from Your Past	Harvey Brown, Jr.
Process Theology: Embracing Adventure with God	Bruce Epperly

Holistic Spirituality: Life Transforming Wisdom from the Letter of James
Bruce Epperly

To Date or Not to Date: What the Bible Says about Pre-Marital Relationships
D. Kevin Brown

The Eucharist: Encounters with Jesus at the Table   Robert D. Cornwall

Forthcoming

God the Creator: The Variety of Christian Views on Origins   Henry Neufeld

The Authority of Scripture in a Postmodern Age: Some Help from Karl Barth
Robert D. Cornwall

Planned

Render to Caesar	Chris Surber
The Caregiver's Beattitudes	Robert Martin
The Problem with Social Justice	Elgin Hushbeck, Jr.
A Cup of Cold Water	Chris Surber
Christian Existentialism	David Moffett-Moore
Paths to Prayer	David Moffett-Moore

(The titles of planned volumes may change before release.)

Generous Quantity Discounts Available
Dealer Inquiries Welcome
Energion Publications — P.O. Box 841
Gonzalez, FL 32560
Website: http://energionpubs.com
Phone: (850) 525-3916

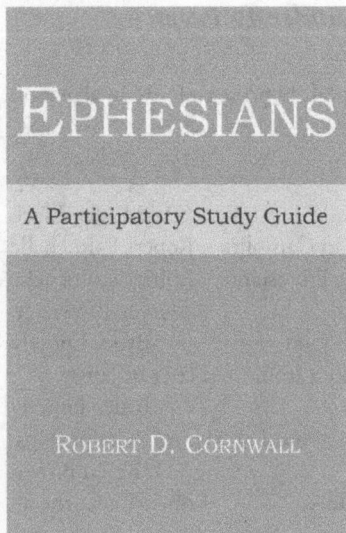

EPHESIANS

A Participatory Study Guide

ROBERT D. CORNWALL

Bob Cornwall combines the mind of a scholar and the heart of a pastor in this participatory study guide on Ephesians.

Dr. Glen Miles
Senior Minister
Country Club Christian Church
(Disciples of Christ)
Kansas City, MO

BY ROBERT D. CORNWALL

The time is now for mainline churches to reappropriate the full spectrum of the spiritual gifts for their contemporary tasks.

Amos Yong, Ph.D.
Dean
Divinity School
Regent University
Author of *Spirit of Love*

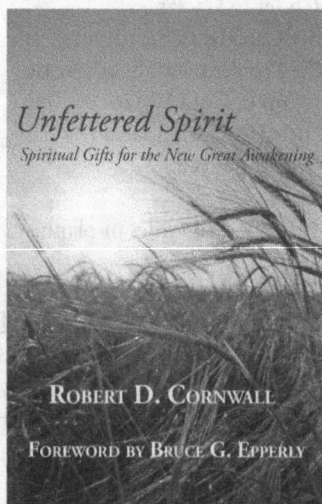

Unfettered Spirit
Spiritual Gifts for the New Great Awakening

ROBERT D. CORNWALL

FOREWORD BY BRUCE G. EPPERLY

More from Energion Publications

Personal Study

Finding My Way in Christianity	Herold Weiss	$16.99
The Jesus Paradigm	David Alan Black	$17.99
When People Speak for God	Henry Neufeld	$17.99

Christian Living

Faith in the Public Square	Robert D. Cornwall	$16.99
Grief: Finding the Candle of Light	Jody Neufeld	$8.99
Crossing the Street	Robert LaRochelle	$16.99

Bible Study

Learning and Living Scripture	Lentz/Neufeld	$12.99
From Inspiration to Understanding	Edward W. H. Vick	$24.99
Luke: A Participatory Study Guide	Geoffrey Lentz	$8.99
Philippians: A Participatory Study Guide	Bruce Epperly	$9.99
Ephesians: A Participatory Study Guide	Robert D. Cornwall	$9.99
Evidence for the Bible	Elgin Hushbeck, Jr.	

Theology

Creation in Scripture	Herold Weiss	$12.99
Creation: the Christian Doctrine	Edward W. H. Vick	$12.99
Ultimate Allegiance	Robert D. Cornwall	$9.99
History and Christian Faith	Edward W. H. Vick	$9.99
The Church Under the Cross	William Powell Tuck	$11.99
The Journey to the Undiscovered Country	William Powell Tuck	$9.99
Eschatology: A Participatory Study Guide	Edward W. H. Vick	$9.99
Philosophy for Believers	Edward W. H. Vick	$14.99
Christianity and Secularism	Elgin Hushbeck, Jr.	$16.99

Ministry

Clergy Table Talk	Kent Ira Groff	$9.99
So Much Older Then …	Robert LaRochelle	$9.99

Generous Quantity Discounts Available
Dealer Inquiries Welcome
Energion Publications — P.O. Box 841
Gonzalez, FL 32560
Website: http://energionpubs.com
Phone: (850) 525-3916

www.ingramcontent.com/pod-product-compliance
Lightning Source LLC
Chambersburg PA
CBHW011750020426
42331CB00014B/3341